DK EYEWITNESS

T0063873

# TOP **10**
# COSTA BLANCA

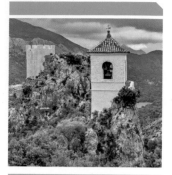

# Top 10 Costa Blanca Highlights

# The Top 10 of Everything

# CONTENTS

## Costa Blanca Area by Area

## Streetsmart

Within each Top 10 list in this book, no hierarchy of quality or popularity is implied. All 10 are, in the editor's opinion, of roughly equal merit.

***Title page, front cover and spine*** *Brightly coloured houses of Villajoyosa*
***Back cover, clockwise from top left*** *Paella with lobsters; the ancient Spanish city of Polop; Catedral de Santa María, Murcia; colourful houses, Villajoyosa; Calp beach*

The rapid rate at which the world is changing is constantly keeping the DK Eyewitness team on our toes. While we've worked hard to ensure that this edition of Costa Blanca is accurate and up-to-date, we know that opening hours alter, standards shift, prices fluctuate, places close and new ones pop up in their stead. So, if you notice we've got something wrong or left something out, we want to hear about it. Please get in touch at **travelguides@dk.com**

# Welcome to the
# Costa Blanca

**Fine beaches, endless sunshine and a lively after-dark scene: these are the best-known draws of the Costa Blanca, but they are only part of the story. Great scenery, good food and monuments galore lend variety to any holiday on this friendly and fascinating coast. With DK Eyewitness Top 10 Costa Blanca, it's yours to explore.**

The Costa Blanca and its southern extension, the Costa Cálida, occupy the middle part of Spain's Mediterranean coast. The cities of **Alicante** (Alacant), set beneath its magnificent castle, and **Murcia**, built around a famous Baroque cathedral, are where most of the action is, but legendary **Benidorm**, an extraordinary cluster of skyscrapers, is the largest and best-known resort here.

Up and down the coast, and inland, there are unmissable sights from all periods of history, including the Gothic mansion of the **Palau Ducal** in Gandia (Gandía), the picturesque mountain village of **Guadalest**, the ancient palm groves of the **Hort del Cura** (Priest's Garden) at Elx (Elche) and Novelda's **Casa-Museo Modernista**, a restored Art Nouveau house.

If you want to get away from it all you can explore the nature reserves of **Calblanque** or **Sierra Espuña**, take a boat trip out to the atmospheric **Isla Tabarca** or climb the **Penyal d'Ifac** (Peñon de Ifach), an extraordinary crag looming over the sea.

Whether you're coming for a weekend or a week, our Top 10 guide brings together the best of everything the region has to offer, from the heaving nightclubs of Benidorm to the wild and lonely heights of the inland sierras. The guide gives you tips throughout, from seeking out what's free to places off the beaten track, plus six easy-to-follow itineraries, designed to help you visit a clutch of sights in a short space of time. Add inspiring photography and detailed maps, and you've got the essential pocket-sized travel companion. **Enjoy the book, and enjoy the Costa Blanca.**

Clockwise from top: **Penyal d'Ifac and Calp (Calpe) beach; La Explanada boulevard Alicante; Altea's blue-domed church, Murcia; castle overlooking Caravaca de la Cruz, Murcia; detail of Murcia casino; Hort del Cura garden, Elx; Catedral de Santa María door, Murcia**

# Exploring the Costa Blanca

The Costa Blanca and the Costa Cálida, and their inland regions, offer an extraordinary variety of sights and scenery. Whether you're here for a short visit or a longer stay, these two-day and seven-day itineraries, starting from the coastal capital of Alicante (Alacant), will guide you round the very best places to visit.

**The pretty whitewashed village of Altea** tumbles down a steep hillside to the Costa Blanca coast.

## Two Days in and around Alicante

### Day ❶

**MORNING**

Take the lift up to the **Castillo de Santa Bárbara** *(see pp14–15)* for a view of the city and of the **Isla Tabarca** *(see pp30–31)* just offshore. After taking the lift back down, stroll along the harbourside **La Explanada** *(see p16)* and through the streets of the old town and the **Barrio de Santa Cruz** *(see p17)*.

**AFTERNOON**

Drive to Novelda to see the Art Nouveau **Casa-Museo Modernista** *(see pp22–3)*, then visit the palm groves of the **Hort del Cura** in Elx (Elche) *(see pp28–9)* before returning to enjoy the nightlife of Alicante.

### Day ❷

**MORNING**

Drive north past the skyscrapers of **Benidorm** *(see p80)*. Stop to take a stroll in the old hilltop town of **Altea** *(see p48)* and then climb or admire the **Penyal d'Ifac** (Peñon de Ifach) *(see pp20–21)* – even the view of it from a distance is spectacular.

**The picturesque mountain village of Guadalest** is topped by castle ruins and overlooks a turquoise reservoir.

**AFTERNOON**

Turn inland to visit the pretty village of **Guadalest** *(see pp18–19)*. Continue through the hills towards **Alcoi** (Alcoy) to pick up the road through **Xixona** (Jijona) back to Alicante *(see pp46–7)*.

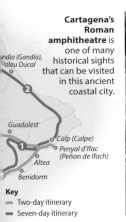

Cartagena's **Roman amphitheatre** is one of many historical sights that can be visited in this ancient coastal city.

**Key**
— Two-day itinerary
— Seven-day itinerary

# Seven Days on the Costa Blanca

## Day ❶
Spend the morning in **Alicante**, visiting the castle (see pp14–15). After lunch, drive up the coast and head inland for **Guadalest** (see pp18–19). Next make your way to **Altea**, and after a stroll round the old town, drive on to **Calp** (Calpe) (see p48).

## Day ❷
Start early to climb the iconic **Penyal d'Ifac** (see pp20–21) and continue north to Gandia (Gandía) to visit the Gothic mansion of the **Palau Ducal** (see pp32–3). A drive west across Valencia brings you to **Xàtiva** (Játiva) (see p81) and its magnificent castle.

## Day ❸
Take the road through **Alcoi** (see p47) and continue along it until you reach the Vinalopó valley. Visit the **Casa-Museo Modernista** in Novelda (see pp22–3). It is then a short trip to the palm groves of the **Hort del Cura** (see pp28–9) in Elx.

## Day ❹
A main road leads from **Elx** (see p91) to **Orihuela** (see p90) and on to **Murcia**. Its Baroque cathedral (see pp34–5) and other monuments deserve a good few hours of sightseeing.

## Day ❺
Set off for **Alhama de Murcia** (see pp27) and explore the wildlife and scenery of the **Sierra Espuña** (see pp26–7). Then head southeast to visit the historical gems in the city of **Cartagena** (see p101).

## Day ❻
Along the coast from **Cartagena** is the seaside nature reserve of **Calblanque** (see pp12–13). After a stroll here, drive around the "inland sea" of the **Mar Menor** (see p101) and then past the salt lagoons of Torrevieja to reach **Santa Pola** (see p89).

## Day ❼
Take the morning ferry to the offshore **Isla Tabarca** (see pp30–31) for a stroll and a picnic. The boat will return you in the afternoon so that you are back in Alicante in time for tapas, dinner and nightlife.

**The Isla Tabarca** is surrounded by the crystal-clear waters of a marine reserve.

# Top 10 Costa Blanca Highlights

Bell tower in the medieval clifftop
village of Guadalest

# 🔟 Costa Blanca Highlights

Sun, sea and sand are excellent reasons to visit the Costa Blanca, but its attractions don't stop there. Inland are Natural Parks, wild sierras, remote hill villages and historic towns. The regional capitals of Alicante (Alacant) and Murcia brim with great shops and tapas bars, while coastal resorts offer lively nightlife. Best of all, there's always a secret cove nearby if the crowds get too much.

## Calblanque ①

Calblanque is a stunning stretch of unspoiled coastline, and one of the area's best-kept secrets. The golden beaches and quiet coves are peaceful even in the height of the tourist season (see pp12–13).

## ② Castillo de Santa Bárbara, Alicante (Alacant)

Visible for miles around, Alicante's castle looms high on a dusty pinnacle. Its ramparts and watchtowers offer spectacular views over the endless blue of the Mediterranean (see pp14–15).

## ③ Guadalest

The enchanting hilltop village of Guadalest sits under romantic castle ruins, and overlooks a beautiful valley with a deep turquoise lake (see pp18–19).

Cast.
Monóvar
Casa-Museo ⑤
Modernista A
Elx (Elche)
Abanilla    Crevillent
Mula    Molina de    Vistabella
Segura
Pliego    Murcia ⑩
Sierra ⑥    Alhama de    San Pedro
España    Murcia    del Pinatar
Funte Alamo    Torre
Lorca    MURCIA    Pacheco
Cartagena    La Unión
Mazarrón    ①
Calblanque

0 km    20
0 miles    20

## ④ Penyal d'Ifac (Peñón de Ifach)

A designated Natural Park, this extraordinary rock erupts spectacularly from the sea over the bay of Calp (Calpe). The views from the summit are breathtaking (see pp20–21).

### 5 Casa-Museo Modernista, Novelda

Every detail of this Art Nouveau-style town house is exquisite, from the sinuous staircase with its vine-leaf motif to the rainbow-coloured skylights (see pp22–3).

### 6 Sierra Espuña

A beautiful stretch of forest and craggy peaks, the Parque Regional de Sierra Espuña offers great hiking, a wealth of wildlife and complete peace (see pp26–7).

### 7 Hort del Cura, Elx (Elche)

This luxuriant garden in the most beautiful corner of the famous palm groves of Elx is a tranquil enclave of tropical flowers and cacti shaded by palm trees (see pp28–9).

### 8 Isla Tabarca

The tiny island of Tabarca is rimmed with rocky coves and fine sandy beaches, and the surrounding marine reserve is a paradise for divers and snorkellers (see pp30–31).

### 9 Palau Ducal, Gandia (Gandía)

This sumptuous Gothic palace was once home to St Francis of Borja (see pp32–3).

### 10 Catedral de Santa María, Murcia

Several centuries in the making, Murcia Cathedral is one of Spain's finest Baroque buildings, with a sumptuous façade and lavishly decorated chapels (see pp34–5).

Alberic
VALENCIA
nals
Llutxent
Gandia (Gandía)
Oliva
imyent
Orba
Dénia (Denia)
Xàbia (Jávea)
Alcoi (Alcoy)
Guadalest
ALICANTE
Penyal d'Ifac (Peñón de Ifach)
Xixone (Jijona)
Benidorm
La Vila Joiosa (Villajoyosa)
Alicante (Alacant)
Isla Tabarca

# 🔟 ⭐ Calblanque

Calblanque, a gorgeous natural paradise near the Mar Menor, is one of the few stretches of Mediterranean coastline to have survived unspoiled – and virtually undiscovered. Over 13 km (8 miles) of quiet coves, sandy beaches and rare fossilized dunes are backed by pine forest and craggy hills, with excellent walking trails offering fine views at every turn. Salt lagoons attract a wealth of birdlife, while the cliffs and hills are home to some unusual species of flora and fauna.

## CALBLANQUE'S "TREE OF LIFE"

A very rare tree grows on the dry, sunny slopes of Calblanque. *Tetraclinis articulata* – the Barbary Arbor-vitae (which translates from the Latin as "tree of life") – only grows in North Africa, Malta and in this part of the Costa Blanca, making it of exceptional interest to botanists. The tree is a kind of cypress and the only species in its genus. It has a conical form, like a cultivated cypress, and is well adapted to conditions in the Mediterranean as it is slow-growing, draught resistant and thrives on thin soils.

### 1 Beaches

Calblanque's beaches are the most beautiful in Murcia **(above)**. Long stretches of golden sand are interspersed with small coves, overlooked by rippling dunes and cliffs. Most popular – yet still not crowded – are Playa de las Cañas, Playa Larga and Playa Calblanque.

### 2 Bird Life

Calblanque is particularly rich in bird life. Among the species you may encounter are Bonelli's eagle, the eagle owl, Audouin's gull and the green woodpecker, as well as flamingoes and several varieties of heron and plover.

### 3 Dunes

Wooden walkways traverse Calblanque's fragile dune system **(below)**, fossilized over millennia and sculpted by wind and sea into spellbinding shapes. The best back onto Cañas, Larga and Negrete Beaches.

### 5 Walks and Rides

The Calblanque Natural Park is covered by a network of walking and mountain-biking trails **(left)**. These are outlined in leaflets you can pick up from the park's information office.

### 6 Coves

The whole coastline is pocked with dozens of tiny coves, where the turquoise waters are perfect for diving and snorkelling. Even in the height of summer you can pick your way across the rocks to find a quiet cove all to yourself.

### 7 Cliffs

Calblanque's rugged yet ethereal cliffs offer spectacular views along the entire coastline.

### 8 Salinas del Rasall

The salt lakes of Rasall still produce salt commercially, and are a major nesting area for resident and migratory birds **(below)**. The waters contain the striped *fartet*, an unusual endangered fish.

### 9 Old Mines

On the outer fringes of Calblanque Park you will see the ghostly remnants of abandoned tin, silver and copper mines.

### 4 Mountain Peaks

The mountains of Calblanque rarely rise above 300 m (984 ft), yet they offer breathtaking views across woods and out to sea.

### 10 Flora and Fauna

In springtime, the hills of Calblanque are carpeted with pretty wild flowers **(above)**. Nestled among the pine forests are rarer trees, including one of the last surviving cypress groves in Spain. Among the fauna, foxes and badgers are common; and several *tortugas bobas* (sea turtles) have been released into the wild along this coast.

# ⭐ Castillo de Santa Bárbara, Alicante (Alacant)

Visible for miles, Alicante's castle looms dramatically above the city. The hill it commands has been inhabited since the Bronze Age, but it was not until the 9th century that the first fortress was built here. Rebuilt during the 16th and 17th centuries, it became a garrison in the 18th century. Its sturdy halls now enclose MUSA, Alicante's history museum. Enter the castle via the Parque de la Ereta, or take the lift.

### MUSA (MUSEO DE LA CIUDAD DE ALICANTE)

The castle houses this museum, which displays different periods in the history of Alicante. The exhibits have been arranged in several buildings throughout this complex, including the old governor's house and the former hospital. Displays range from ancient Roman and Greek artifacts to medieval maps and armour. You can also visit the 16th-century *aljibes*, deep wells dug in the rock to store water.

**Castillo de Santa Bárbara, Alicante**

### 1 Plaza del Cuartel

This wide, sun-bleached expanse at the centre of the fortress is dominated by the massive former *cuartel* (barracks building), which contains an exhibition on the castle's development. Nearby, the snack kiosk and picnic area offer fine views.

### 2 Lift

If you can't face the climb to the top of the hill, this lift will swoop you up in seconds into the heart of the castle. Tunnelled through the rock, its entrance is opposite the Postiguet Beach below.

### 3 Macho del Castillo

The highest point of the whole complex is the Macho del Castillo, a wide square that offers the most spectacular views of all **(above)**. It is still scattered with rusting cannons, which poke through the fortifications in all directions.

### 7 Solid Fortress

Perched high on Monte Benacantil, Alicante's castle is one of the largest surviving castles in Spain, an impressive complex of sturdy stone halls and courtyards **(left)** built over 900 years.

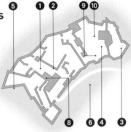

**Castillo de Santa Bárbara**

### 4 Parque de Ingenieros

Shaded with palms and scattered with wooden benches, the Parque de Ingenieros (Engineers' Park) is the prettiest and greenest of the castle's squares.

### 5 Ramparts and Terraces

You can stroll along vast sections of the massive fortifications, which still encircle the castle. The views are spectacular.

### 6 Parks

The road up to the castle winds through the pine-shaded Parque Monte Benacantil. On the southern side, the award-winning Parque de la Ereta includes a restaurant, an open-air café and an exhibition hall.

### 8 Antiguo Cuerpo de Guardia

In the 18th century, the castle tavern and the guardroom used to share this building – guard duty must have been popular! Now it contains galleries.

### 10 Cuartel de Ingenieros

One of the largest of the castle buildings, the Engineers' Barracks – erected in the 1700s – is now a stunning gallery for art exhibitions, and also offers splendid views.

### 9 La Torreta

Poised over the main entrance to the castle, this watchtower is its oldest structure, and includes stones from the original Arab fortress **(above)**.

---

**NEED TO KNOW**

**MAP E5** ■ Monte Benacantil; www.castillode santabarbara.com

*Castle Complex:* 673 84 98 90; open 10am–6pm daily (Mar–mid-Jun: to 8pm; mid-Jun–early Sep: to 11pm); lift ticket: €2.70 (free for under 5s & over 65s)

*MUSA (Museo de la Ciudad de Alicante):* open 10am–2:30pm & 4–8pm daily; guided tours available

■ Within the castle complex, the Cafeteria Santa Barbara offers a variety of food at reasonable prices. Open daily.

■ The lift takes you up to the castle, but stroll back down to enjoy the two parks along the way.

■ The castle complex has no information office, but maps are available within the galleries.

■ There is wheelchair access to the lift and central square only.

# Other Sights in Alicante (Alacant)

Impressive façade of Alicante's Baroque town hall

### 1 Ayuntamiento
**MAP U2** ■ Plaza del Ayuntamiento ■ 966 90 08 86 ■ Open 9am–2pm Mon–Fri

Alicante's grand town hall is the city's finest Baroque building.

### 2 La Explanada
**MAP U3**

The famous, palm-lined boulevard of La Explanada is paved with an attractive undulating marble mosaic. It's a favourite place for the evening stroll *(paseo)*.

### 3 Concatedral de San Nicolás
**MAP U2** ■ C/Labradores ■ 965 21 26 62 ■ Open 7:30am–1pm & 5:30–8:30pm Mon–Fri, 8:30am–1pm & 5:30–9pm Sat & Sun

The hulking 17th-century cathedral dominates Alicante's old quarter.

### 4 The Old Town (El Barrio)
**MAP U2**

Built around the slopes of Monte Benacantil, this area is attractive at any time of day or night.

**Tile from Concatedral de San Nicolas**

### 5 MARQ (Museo Arqueológico Provincial de Alicante)
**MAP V1** ■ Plaza Dr Gómez Ulla s/n ■ 965 14 90 00 ■ Open Jul & Aug: 10am–11pm Tue–Sun & public hols; Sep–Jun: 10am–7pm Tue–Fri, 10am–8:30pm Sat, 10am–2pm Sun & public hols ■ www.marqalicante.com ■ Adm

This high-tech, hands-on museum spans prehistory to contemporary times.

### 6 Basílica de Santa María
**MAP V2** ■ Plaza de Santa María ■ 965 21 60 26 ■ Open 10am–1pm & 6–7:30pm daily

Alicante's oldest and prettiest church.

### 7 Lucentum
**MAP E5** ■ C/Zeus, Playa de la Albufereta ■ 965 14 90 00 ■ Open 10am–2pm & 4–6pm Tue–Sat, 10am–2pm Sun; mid-Jun–mid-Sep: 9am–noon & 7–10pm Tue–Sat, 9am–noon Sun ■ www.marqalicante.com ■ Adm

In Roman times, Lucentum was a sizeable trading centre. Only these evocative ruins by the sea remain.

### 3 MUBAG (Museo de Bellas Artes)

MAP V2 ■ C/Gravina 13–15 ■ Open Jul & Aug: 11am–9pm Tue–Sat (until 3pm Sun & public hols); Sep–Jun: 10am–8pm (until 2pm Sun & public hols) ■ www.mubag.es

A fine art collection displayed in Palacio Conde Lumiares *(see p40)*.

### 9 Monasterio de la Santa Faz

MAP E5 ■ Ctra de Valencia ■ 965 26 49 12 ■ Open 10am–2pm Mon–Thu, 11am–6pm Fri, 8am–2pm Sun

This monastery is said to contain a fragment of the Holy Shroud. A pilgrimage takes place after Easter Sunday.

### 10 Barrio de Santa Cruz
MAP U2

Alicante's oldest quarter has charming houses and flower-filled balconies.

**The flower-filled Barrio de Santa Cruz**

## LAS HOGUERAS DE SAN JUAN

The fabulous fiery festival of Las Hogueras (Foguers in Valenciano), the biggest on the Alicante calendar, culminates on 24 June, the feast day of St John the Baptist. The festival begins with a bang – literally – on 20 June, with "La Mascletà", an ear-splitting barrage of fire-crackers. Each neighbourhood vies to create the best *hoguera*, an enormous colourful wax or papier-mâché figure. At midnight on 24 June, after a spectacular fireworks display from the top of the castle, all of the *hogueras* are set on fire – even the winning entry. There are folk parades, medieval markets and fire-cracker competitions throughout the week.

**Colourful figure at the festival of Las Hogueras**

**TOP 10 OTHER FESTIVALS IN ALICANTE**

**1** Mid-Jan: Porrate de San Antón (traditional fair)

**2** Feb: Carnavales (Carnival)

**3** Easter: Semana Santa (Holy Week)

**4** Second Thu after Easter Sunday: Peregrinación de la Santa Faz (pilgrimage)

**5** End of Apr: Moros y Cristianos (mock battles)

**6** May: Cruces de Mayo (flower competition)

**7** 16 July: Virgen del Carmen (sailors' festival)

**8** Jul, Aug: Fiestas de Verano (music, dance and theatre)

**9** 3 Aug: Virgen del Remedio (festival dedicated to one of Alicante's patron saints)

**10** 6 Dec: Fiesta de San Nicolás (another patron saint of the city)

# 🔟⭐ Guadalest

The tiny village of Guadalest is a spectacular sight, perched on a lofty crag and topped by the ruins of a medieval castle. Its picture-postcard allure draws crowds of day-trippers, yet Guadalest retains its medieval charm. The upper village is accessed by a tunnel hewn through the rock; beneath is the sprawl of the old Muslim quarter, with a string of souvenir shops and cafés. The view from the castle walls at the top of the village extends all the way down to the coast.

**The fairy-tale village of Guadalest**

## ① Puerta de San José

The *puerta* (entrance) to the upper village is a tiny arch leading to a tunnel hollowed out of the rock. Pass through it to emerge onto a cobbled street.

## ② Castillo de San José

Almost nothing survives of the medieval castle, but the romantic ruins offer superb views of the surrounding countryside **(below)**. The entrance is via the Casa Orduña, where a stone path ends in the battered towers of the original fortress.

**NEED TO KNOW**

**MAP F3**

*Tourist Office:* Avda de Alicante s/n; 965 88 52 98; open 10:30am–2pm & 3–5:30pm Sun–Fri; www. guadalest.es

*Casa Orduña:* C/Iglesia 2; 965 88 53 93; open summer: 10:15am–8pm daily, winter: 10am–6pm daily; adm: €4 (includes castle entrance)

*Casa Típica:* C/Iglesia 1; 661 15 27 74; open 10am–7pm Sun–Fri; donation requested for entrance

*Museo de Microminiaturas:* C/Iglesia 5; 965 88 50 62; open 10am–8pm (until 6pm in winter) daily; adm: €4

■ There are lots of cafés in the Plaza San de Gregorio (upper village). The best restaurant in the area is Xortà at Ctra Callosa-Alcoi (965 88 51 87; open Tue–Sun L). It serves delicious roast lamb. Diners can also enjoy views of the valley.

**Guadalest**

**HISTORY OF GUADALEST**

First built by the Arabs around AD 715, little Guadalest used to be an important military outpost. The castle was conquered and expanded by Christian armies under Jaime I in 1238, before it was damaged and then ruined by earthquakes in 1644 and 1748 respectively.

### 6 Casa Orduña

The grandest house in Guadalest, this imposing residence, once home to the Orduña family, appears to cling onto the cliff face. It still retains many of its original 18th- and 19th-century furnishings, paintings and *objets d'art*. The upper levels contain an art gallery.

### 8 Casa Típica

Take a glimpse into Guadalest's domestic and agricultural past in this reconstruction of a late-18th-century farmhouse complete with costumes and scale models of farm equipment.

### 3 Bell Tower

The whitewashed bell tower is a beloved symbol of Guadalest. From high above the village, its low chimes echo across the valley.

### 7 Embalse de Guadalest

This vast turquoise *embalse* (reservoir) provides water for the parched coastal regions. It's also the perfect spot for a picnic **(above)**.

### 4 Plaza de San Gregorio

The only street in the upper village leads to the Plaza de San Gregorio, with a statue **(right)**, shops, cafés, and a fantastic viewing point (*mirador*) overlooking the beautiful reservoir below.

### 9 Cemetery

High up in the village is a tiny, neglected cemetery – the highest in Spain. It's scattered with a motley collection of limbless statues, and offers more breathtaking views over the valley.

### 5 Museo de Microminiaturas

Guadalest is full of quirky museums; the Museo de Microminiaturas is the strangest. Its treasures are viewed through magnifying glasses, and include the Eiffel Tower sculpted on the head of a pin, and Velázquez's *Las Meninas* painted on a grain of corn.

### 10 Gifts and Souvenirs

Guadalest has many gift shops selling lace, local honey, fiery local spirits and the usual tourist fare.

# **TOP 10** ⭐ Penyal d'Ifac (Peñón de Ifach)

This sheer, impregnable crag dominating the bay of Calp (Calpe) is the iconic symbol of the Costa Blanca. Once a pirate hideout, it's now a Natural Park perfumed with lavender and wild flowers. A steep trail zigzags upward, cuts through a tunnel in the rock, then winds dramatically to a viewing point at the summit, 332 m (1,089 ft) above sea level. A word of caution: the first section of the trail is suitable for walkers of all levels; after the tunnel, it becomes increasingly tricky.

**1 Summit of Ifac**
The narrow hiking trail leads to the very top of the rock, with stunning views of distant mountain ranges, the coastline and far out to sea.

**2 Tunnel**
In 1918, a tunnel was cut through the rock to ease the climb **(above)**. It is steep, but visitors are no longer hauled over the cliff face by rope, as was the old custom.

**4 Miradors**
There are several *miradors* (viewing points) on the rock, but the best views (besides those from the summit) are probably from the old guard post on the southern flank.

**5 Climbing Routes**
A rock-climbers' mecca, the Penyal d'Ifac has several climbing routes on both the north and south faces, which take between 5 and 11 hours.

**3 Hiking Trail**
On the lower flanks of the rock, the main trail to the summit twists and turns through gnarled pine trees and swathes of perfumed lavender. On the upper reaches, you'll need a head for heights and sturdy footwear **(right)**.

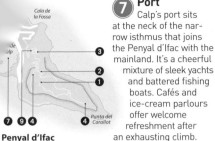

Penyal d'Ifac

### 7 Port

Calp's port sits at the neck of the narrow isthmus that joins the Penyal d'Ifac with the mainland. It's a cheerful mixture of sleek yachts and battered fishing boats. Cafés and ice-cream parlours offer welcome refreshment after an exhausting climb.

### 6 Coves and Inlets

The base of the Penyal d'Ifac is dotted with picturesque coves, which also have protected status under the Natural Park scheme. A real paradise for divers and snorkellers, the crystal-clear waters are home to a wealth of marine life.

**The Penyal d'Ifac in Calp bay**

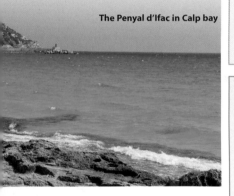

### 8 Flora and Fauna

There are more than 300 species of flora on the scrubby slopes of Ifac, including lavender, goldenrod and red valerian. The rarest plants are contained in two microreserves. Few animals, besides lizards and other reptiles, can survive the parched conditions.

### 9 Exhibition

A cluster of buildings at the base of the Penyal d'Ifac contains the park information office and two exhibition rooms, which highlight the most important features of the park and describe the wildlife within its borders.

### 10 Birds

The Penyal d'Ifac is home to more than 80 species of bird, including the northern gannet, Eleanora's falcon, the peregrine falcon, the shag and several species of gull **(left)**.

## THE PENYAL UNDERWATER

The Penyal d'Ifac is as fascinating under water as it is above; octopuses and scorpion fish lurk in the shadows, and dive-through tunnels feature colourful anemones. Several companies offer beginners' diving courses and dives around the rock. These include Club Nautico Les Basetes (Ctra Calpe-Moraira Km 2, Benissa; 965 83 12 13; cnlesbasetes.com); Dive & Dive (Avda del Port 14, Calp; 965 83 92 70 or 607 61 96 30; www.divedivecompany.com); and Scuba 4 You (Partida Calalga 30, Calp; 605 83 04 14).

## NEED TO KNOW

**MAP G4 ■ Calp (Calpe)**

*Visitor Information Centre:* Av de los Ejércitos Españoles 44, Calp; 965 83 69 20; open Mar–Sep: 9am–2:30pm Mon & Wed–Fri (from 9:30am Sat, Sun & public hols), Oct–Feb: 8:30am–2:30pm Mon–Fri (from 9:30am Sat, Sun & public hols)

■ There are no cafés, but picnics are permitted so long as you collect all your rubbish. The nearby port has several cafés.

■ The number of visitors on the rock is strictly limited, with a maximum of 150 allowed to climb it at any one time. In high season, arrive early in the day, and try to avoid weekends if you want to dodge the queues.

■ The information centre is at the park's entrance.

# ★ Casa-Museo Modernista, Novelda

Anyone who has admired Antoni Gaudí's buildings in Barcelona will love this lavish Art Nouveau-style town house, with swirling wood-work, delicate wrought iron and turn-of-the-20th-century furnishings. It belonged to Antonia Navarro, a young widow with a large fortune, and was designed by the celebrated Murcian architect Pedro Cerdán. It fell into disrepair after the Civil War, but a meticulous restoration project has returned the graceful salons to their former glory.

### 1 Façade
The façade fuses Classical lines and Modernista details: wrought-iron balconies, stone fruit and flowers, and rosy marble panels.

### 3 Dining Room
This lavish room **(below)** contains frescoes of languid women in woodland settings, elaborately trimmed doorways, and carved furniture.

### 2 Study
The study is full of exquisitely carved wood-work, from the sculpted leaves on the fireplace to the undulating panelling on the lower walls.

### 4 Gallery
The exceptional woodwork featured all over the house reaches its height in the lavish wooden gallery, which encloses the stairwell.

### 5 Patio/Courtyard
The delightful, ivy-draped patio is lined with pale sculpted columns supporting fine arches **(above)**. Hand-painted tiles depict Antonia Navarro's substantial country estates.

### 6 Ballroom
The ballroom is a theatrical whirl of red and gold. It features an exquisite tiled floor, designed by renowned Catalan architect Lluís Domènech i Montaner.

---

**NEED TO KNOW**

**MAP D5**

*Casa-Museo Modernista:* C/Mayor 24, Novelda; 965 60 02 37; open 10am–1:30pm Tue–Fri; closed Sat–Mon

*Novelda tourist office:* C/Mayor 6; 965 60 92 28

■ There is no café in the building, but you can enjoy local delicacies at ou Cucuch restaurant

and tapas bar on C/Argentina 18 (965 60 30 34; open Tue–Sat & Sun L).

■ The house has no lift and limited wheelchair access.

■ Modernista architecture fans can also visit Novelda's Casino on C/Emilio Castelar s/n (965 60 00 30), and the nearby Santuario de Santa María Magdalena on Cerro de la Mola.

### 7 Staircase

The marble staircase curves and curls sinuously upward, an intricate garland of wrought-iron vine tendrils curling between the balusters. Carved wooden panels succeed each other like waves. The bannister ends in a graceful lamp at the foot of the stairs.

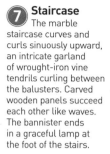

**Casa-Museo Modernista**

**Key to Floorplan**
- Ground floor
- First floor

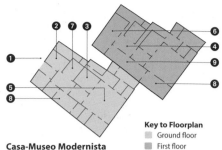

### 10 Stained-Glass Ceilings

The entrance hall is flooded with light from a spectacular stained-glass ceiling **(above)**. Over the stairwell, a smaller, even more extravagant stained-glass ceiling can be found surrounded by ceramic flowers and exuberant plasterwork.

### 8 Bedrooms

All of the house's bedrooms have original furnishings **(below)**. The bathroom adjoining the main bedroom has a huge bath carved from a single slab of marble.

### 9 Exhibitions

The house has two permanent exhibitions: one of Art Nouveau-style graphic design; the other dedicated to Novelda-born 18th-century explorer Jorge Juan.

**THE MODERNISTAS**

Modernista architecture is noted for its organic forms, flowing lines and elaborate decoration. It celebrated the traditional crafts of woodcarving, stonemasonry and ceramic tiling, but used them in new ways. The most famous Modernista architect was Gaudí. His spellbinding buildings in Barcelona inspired many architects in the Costa Blanca, who used his revolutionary ideas of colour and form in their beautiful new mansions and public buildings.